ROBERT A. CHESEBROUGH'S

SYSTEM OF LOCOMOTION

FOR

ELEVATED RAILROADS.

PATENTED JULY 14, 1868.

LETTER

OF

GEN. EGBERT L. VIELE, C. E.

New York:
C. S. WESTCOTT & CO., PRINTERS,
No. 79 John Street.
1869.

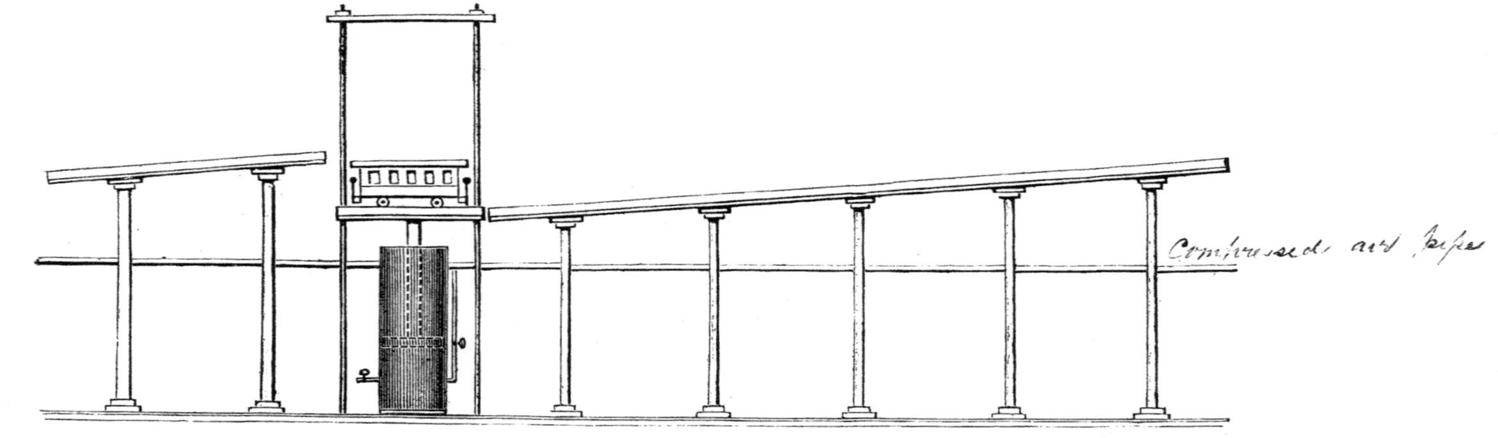
Compressed air pipe

LETTER OF GENERAL E. L. VIELE, C. E.

ELEVATED RAILROADS.

NEW YORK, *November* 16, 1868.

To the Editor of the Herald:

Perhaps of all others the most urgent need of New York to-day is frequent, speedy, reliable, and cheap means of communication with the upper part of the island. This attained, the future of our city is destined to be one of unexampled growth, grandeur, and prosperity. During the last few years the attention of engineers has been called to this subject and its growing importance, and a variety of plans have been laid before the people and the State Legislature. Of these plans the most prominent presented have been the arcade, the depressed, the underground, and an elevated road, to be worked by a series of cables. The public have been informed already through the press of the design and method of construction proposed in these several plans, two of which—viz., the underground and elevated cable roads—were chartered by the Legislature last winter, and arrangements are now progressing for their construction. My special object at present, however, is to lay before your readers a novel plan of a railroad for New York, which during my investigations of the subject has but recently come under my notice, and which seems to me to possess some considerable merit. This invention proposes an elevated railroad, the track of which consists of a series of inclined planes, down which a car runs by its own gravity, elevating platforms being interposed to raise the car from the foot of one incline to the head of the next. In other words, the car runs down hill all the way, being elevated to the top of the succeeding hill when the bottom of the first is reached. The elevating platforms are to be operated by compressed air, which lifts a piston-head working perpendicularly in an upright cylinder, the platform being attached directly to the piston-rod and kept in its proper place by guides. The air is compressed at the end of the route by a stationary engine, operating powerful air-pumps, which force the compressed air into a large iron boiler or receiver. To this receiver is attached an ordinary steam pipe of say two inches in diameter, which runs the entire length of the road, and is provided with the necessary branch pipes and valves to connect with each of the elevators and supply the compressed air to them as required. The pressure throughout the length of the pipe will be constantly the same as in the receiver. Supposing a car to weigh three thousand pounds and hold forty passengers, the total weight to be raised would be about nine thousand five hundred pounds. Now, if the diameter of the cylinder of each elevator should be twenty inches, the number of square inches contained in the piston-head would be nearly four hundred, and, with fifty pounds pressure of air to the square inch, the lifting force would be nearly twenty thousand pounds, or more than twice the force required. This would insure rapid elevation, and it is claimed by the inventor that the platforms holding loaded cars could be elevated at a speed equal to one foot per second of time. That a car will descend an inclined plane by its own gravity is undoubted, and that this mode of progression is superior to others on many accounts (where it can be practically used) can scarcely be questioned. The points to be determined in this connection are: What grade does the incline require? and can that grade be obtained without starting from an elevation which would render the whole plan impracticable? After a high degree of momentum has been once obtained by the car, a very slight descent will suffice to keep up its speed; but in order to obtain speed rapidly from the start the descent of the grade must be considerably greater. This can be provided for by regulating the grade of the inclines on a sliding scale, commencing with (for example) a grade of sixty feet to the mile, and reducing the scale to nearly a dead level at the end of the section. The necessity for a steep grade on the start may, however, be removed by using some mechanical means of starting the car quickly, and to effect this the following is proposed by the inventor: After a loaded car has been elevated, attach a rope, with a ring on the end of it, into a hook, fastened on the under part of the car; this rope runs along the track some fifty feet, then over a loose pulley, and to it is attached an iron weight of say one thousand pounds, which is suspended from it, sliding down oiled guides to the ground. The brakes being loosened, the car immediately starts forward down the incline, its speed accelerated by the steady dead weight of one thousand pounds. The power of this weight is retained for fifty feet, or until the loose pulley is reached, when the ring slides off the hook (its direction being changed), and the car proceeds rapidly alone on its descent. The weight is immediately hoisted again into position by the descending platform for a succeeding car. To effect an immediate descent of the elevating platform, the air contained in the cylinders, after the compressed air has been let out, may be exhausted by having a second pipe running the entire length of the road, connecting with an exhausted receiver, from which the air has been removed by an air-pump, worked by the same engine which operates the compressing-pumps. By this means a total vacuum could not be obtained, but an exhaustive force of about eight pounds to the square inch could easily be obtained, which would suck the platform down instantly with a weight of air upon it of over three thousand pounds, in addition to the actual weight of the platform. This would insure the immediate ascent of the one thousand pounds weight, ready to be attached to the succeeding car at the summit of the plane. By using these or some other means, such, perhaps, as a velocipede or lever movement, it is claimed that cars could follow each other as rapidly as one in every two minutes with perfect safety. On the Erie Railroad it has been found that a train running down a grade of thirty feet to the mile will acquire a speed so great as to require an almost constant application of the brakes. It is therefore probable, that should a proper means of starting the car be adopted, it will be found that a grade beginning at forty feet to the mile and running down almost to a level will be ample. In order to show what elevation would be necessary, and what would be the gradual descent of grade for such a track, the following table is submitted. The sections are supposed to be one mile long, and the lowest point of the track twelve and one-half feet above the street:

TABLE OF MILE SECTIONS.

On the 1st 1,000 ft.,	allow a fall of	8 ft.,	equal to grade of	42¼ ft.	to the mile.
" 2d 1,000 "	"	5 "	"	26⅜ "	"
" 3d 1,000 "	"	3½ "	"	18⅜ "	"
" 4th 1,000 "	"	2½ "	"	13¼ "	"
Last 1,280 "	"	2 "	"	8¼ "	"
One mile, 5,280 "	Total fall,	21 "			
	Elevation above street.....	12½ "			
	Elevation of highest point..	33½ "			

Elevation of lowest point, 12½ feet.

Should it, however, be deemed advisable to locate the stations, which are situated at the end of the sections, one-half mile apart instead of one mile apart, as in the above table, it is evident the same grade can be retained and still the total fall reduced to one-half of twenty-one feet, viz.:

TABLE OF HALF-MILE SECTIONS.

On the 1st 500 feet	allow a fall of	4 ft.,	equal to grade of	42¼ ft.	to the mile.
" 2d 500	"	2½	"	26⅜	"
" 3d 500	"	1¾	"	18⅜	"
" 4th 500	"	1¼	"	13¼	"
Last 640	"	1	"	8¼	"
Half-mile 2,640	Total fall,	10½			
	Elevation above street,	12½			
	Elevation of highest point,	23			

Elevation of lowest point, 12½ feet.

The cost of building the track at an elevation of from 23 feet to 12½ feet, will of course be very much less than building it at an elevation of from $33\frac{1}{2}$ feet to $12\frac{1}{2}$ feet. The route should be selected on a line as free as possible from differences in elevation, or if the surface lies in short, wavy lines, two points might be selected of nearly the same height, at the proper distances for stations, and ordinary depressions or elevations between those points would not then be so important. Should, however, the road be built on the streets fronting the two rivers, a level would be obtained all around the island, or nearly so. The structure need not be built so massively as at first glance might appear to be necessary. Where locomotive power or traction ropes are used, the jar, resistance, wear, and friction are very great, but in a gravity road of this character, the track being true and well oiled, the friction would be but little and the weight to be sustained small, as the cars proceed singly. In the construction of the road it is claimed that a single line of iron columns, running on each side of the street, and braced transversely across the street by iron girders and longitudinally to each other, said columns being thirty feet apart, would be sufficiently strong to hold up two tracks, one running north and the other south, on opposite sides of the street. The columns to have broad flat bases resting on solid masonry foundations, and to have branches jutting off into the earth, just below the surface, which should be laid in cement, in such a way that the columns could neither sink nor incline. Whether this mode of construction would be preferable to laying the track on light trellis work on each side of the street would be a question for the constructing engineer after deciding upon the line of the route. Some simple means of preventing a car from leaving the track in case of accident should be adopted, although precautions of this character would almost seem to be unnecessary, as the road would be nearly straight, the flanges of the wheels deep, and the absence of all force, jerking, or sudden starting would make it difficult to throw a car off a properly constructed track. The cars may be warmed with hot water contained in pipes running through them, which may be replenished from a tank at the end of the route after each trip. Passengers enter and leave the car, after it has run down the incline on to the elevating platform, by a staircase and gate, leading twelve and one-half feet up from the street; they are then elevated in the car to the head of the incline. It seems hardly possible that any system could be devised by which cars could be run at anything like the cost of operating this road. It is claimed that but two men would be needed at each stopping station, one to take the fares and another to operate the elevator ; and each car would require but one man to work the brakes, of which there should be two distinct sets. The cost of operating the road would therefore be so small that the fare could be put at such a low rate as to be within the means for daily use of the working classes, and stockholders would receive the principal part of the receipts, instead of having them absorbed in running expenses. The inventor also claims that this mode of transit can be applied to suspension bridges, connecting different banks of rivers, one elevator on each end of the bridge being alone required to operate the road. Passengers could in this way be carried over long bridges at great speed and at a trifling cost. Also that this system is well adapted to short, or even long roads, for moving freight from point to point where the surface of the ground is not too irregular. In the country or in towns, where the roadway could be purchased, the track could run down to the ground, thus avoiding the additional elevation of twelve and a half feet above the street needed in cities ; and as in many circumstances high speed might not be required, the grades of the inclines might be materially reduced, thus cheapening the cost of erection. Also that for cross-town transit from river to river in New York independent sections of a road on this plan could be built at various points, and would meet a growing necessity. Air follows a fixed law of compression up to twenty-seven atmospheres, and beyond that is compressible without limit. It is also unlimitedly expansible. These features, it is claimed, render it the most desirable power for the present purpose. Steam engines might be employed to raise the elevators, or steam might be injected directly into the cylinders, but it seems to me, after some consideration, that the use of compressed air would be better in all respects. Its action is instantaneous and unchecked by the condensation that steam is subject to: the air-pipes can neither rust nor freeze; the movement is swift, steady, and irresistible, the power being only limited by the size of the cylinder and the pressure per square inch. The platform could not fall even should the cylinder leak badly, for the descent would then be no faster than through the opening of the air-valve, and the car would rest on a bed, which for elasticity could not be excelled by springs. One boiler and engine runs the entire road on both sides of the street, and is situated at the extreme end of the route. I do not know that there is any table by which the speed that a car will acquire on a certain incline can be ascertained, and it seems difficult to determine a point which is dependent for solution on so many surrounding circumstances, such as the weight of the car, size of the wheels, regularity and length of the track, condition of the bearings and springs, and lubrication of the track and axles. If the road should be carefully constructed and all these points looked to, it seems reasonable to conclude that a high rate of speed could be quickly obtained. I am not aware that an ordinary gravity road has ever been constructed with a view of obtaining all the speed the decline would admit of; consequently this point may be said to be undetermined. The conformation of New York island is such that a route from Harlem bridge to City Hall could be selected, which would answer for this plan. The building of the road is simple, and I cannot find that it offers to the engineer any mechanical difficulty to overcome; and two points in its favor are the rapidity with which it could be constructed and its cheapness compared with some other plans. In the future New York will need all the communication between the upper and lower part of the island which can be furnished, and a supply of that need will but create increased demand for it. It is proposed that the running time between City Hall and Harlem bridge shall not exceed twenty-five minutes. The objections of civil engineers to the plan are respectfully invited by the inventor and patentee, Mr. Robert A. Chesebrough, of this city.

EGBERT L. VIELE.

A RAILROAD FOR NEW YORK.

The question which meets us at the start, is what kind of a road is best adapted to the wants of New York. There is a choice of three ways of travel: on the surface, under the surface, and above the surface. The first way may be dismissed without argument. Surface horse roads have proved entirely inadequate to the necessities of New York, and each year their inability to meet the demands of travel becomes more apparent. Nor can they be increased to any important extent. After a heavy fall of snow, travel on these roads is always delayed and impeded, and occasionally totally suspended; and at such times, it is an economy of time, patience, and suffering to walk, rather than trust oneself to the inside of a horse car. There is but one way to relieve the city by surface roads, and that is to resign one avenue on each side of Broadway to the exclusive use of steam railroads, fencing them in the entire distance, and station flagmen at the gates, necessary at the crossings. There are so many substantial objections to this plan that it will scarcely be adopted, except as a last resort, and we will not therefore now further consider it.

The second way of travel is by

AN UNDER-GROUND STEAM ROAD.

There are three plans proposed for sub-surface roads, viz.: The tunnel, the arcade, and the depressed, all of which differ materially in their mode of construction, and the principal features of which are generally understood by the public. The first objection to an under-ground road is the great cost. The cost of the London tunnel was $5,000,000 or more per mile, and it is not believed that one could be built in New York for less than that sum. The value of the property which would have to be paid for, and destroyed to provide a sufficient number of open cuts for ventilation, would be immense, and even then under the most advantageous circumstances, the close air of a tunnel would simply be bearable, not inviting. The arcade plan is magnificent in design, but so radical in character and proposes changes of so important a nature for our principal thoroughfare as to demand the most complete investigation before adoption. If the results promised by the distinguished engineer who planned it should be obtained, they would well pay for the outlay, and Broadway would become the most beautiful avenue in the world; but who believes if work was commenced to-morrow on the arcade road, that it could be completed to Central Park. certainly not to Harlem River, in ten years, and meantime New York goes afoot. The depressed railroad contemplates the purchase of private property along its entire line. If the difficulty of purchasing this property at the high value of New York real estate could be surmounted, this road could undoubtedly be built at much less cost than either of the others, and would, as far as running is concerned, be far better than the tunnel plan, but it would seem that the difficulty of purchasing a line of private property over thirty feet wide through the heart of New York, to be used for steam engines, will prove insuperable.

The third way of travel is through the air, by

AN ELEVATED RAILROAD.

The great difficulty in the way of this plan has been the want of a motive power which would afford rapid speed at low cost, and be unobjectionable. This furnished the rest becomes easy. The cost of its construction is trifling compared with the cost of any of the plans referred to. The right of way costs nothing, destroys no property, and interferes with no other interests. The road can never be blockaded or impeded, and all weathers are the same to it. As to its safety, when closely examined the danger is imaginary, not real. On surface roads, cars leave the track because there is no depth to the rail or length to the flange of the wheel, purposely so arranged to prevent injury to the wheels of vechicles using the street. On the elevated road the track could be raised several inches, and the wheels be made with double flanges two or three times the ordinary depth, which would make it impossible for a car to run off. One hundred heavy trains per day cross Harlem flats, after leaving the tunnel at Yorkville, on a narrow causeway over fifty feet high with perfect safety, and yet the place is tenfold more dangerous than would be an elevated street track properly constructed. If the motive power used should be of such a nature that it will gradually impair the strength of the structure, or absolutely jerk the car off the track, the difficulty developed is with the power used, not the road, and this point is really the only one at issue.

THE MOTIVE POWER.

Several plans of locomotion are proposed: *First*, by a propelling endless cable; *Second*, by the use of improved dummy engines; and, *Third*, by locating on each car an air engine and a tank of air compressed to a high pressure to operate the engine; the tank to be replenished at the several stations.

In regard to the first plan, we will simply say that the objections urged against it are various, and some of them undoubtedly well grounded. If it succeeds, it will be by the determined perseverance and energy of its undaunted projector in the face of serious obstacles, and the almost unanimous adverse opinion of the engineering profession. As to the second plan it is at least feasible, and a certain power, but expensive and objectionable. The escaping smoke and steam will be a constant source of annoyance. If trains are run, the entire structure would have to be massively built to allow for increased weight, friction, and depreciation; in fact, the entire character of the road would have to be different from what we propose, but if the cars are run singly and a light dummy attached to each, it will be readily seen that the cost of such transportation would render a high fare necessary to make the road self-supporting. As to the third plan: it would be the one "*par excellence*" if it could be persuaded to work. Compressed air as a motive power is better than steam for intermittent use, if during the intervals of use its exhausted power is restored; but as a power for continuous use, its use will be hardly practical, unless the restorative force is also continuous or nearly so. Power cannot be increased in amount by mechanical devices; for every pound of power obtained from compressed air, the same amount of force must be expended in compressing it. The use of air in the way proposed, compressed to a much greater pressure than one hundred pounds to the square inch, will scarcely be found practical; it is folly to talk of charging tanks with air at a pressure of five hundred to six hundred pounds to the square inch, by means of flexible and changeable connections, to be adjusted and removed every few minutes. This idea is a threadbare one, and has generations ago cost the credulous dearly. But air at a reasonable pressure can undoubtedly be used, and so far as it will go, will be a first-class power; but at every stroke of the engine the power becomes weaker, and would be entirely gone before a car could travel a thousand feet, for no tank which a passenger car could conveniently carry would contain enough air to last its journey between stations. For stationary power the use of air is practical, for locomotion we do not believe it to be so, except in the manner hereafter described. We therefore come to the present system of operating, which we claim removes the objections to an elevated road, by furnishing reliable and certain motive power.

CHESEBROUGH'S SYSTEM OF LOCOMOTION

Consists in constructing a track on a series of inclined planes, down which each car runs successively by its own gravity, and on reaching the bottom of one incline it runs on to an elevating platform, by which it is raised to the head of the next incline, and so continues on its journey. (See plate.) At first glance it might seem that the elevations would require to be great and frequent, but by reference to the table in the preceding letter, it will be seen that an elevation of ten and a half feet to every half mile will be sufficient to develop high speed, used in connection with some simple car starting apparatus. The preceding letter of General Egbert L. Viele, published in the "New York Herald" of November 18, 1868, enters so fully into the details of the method of operating the road that but little remains to be explained in relation thereto; and the inventor here desires to acknowledge the obligation he is under to General Viele, who, without fee, or the hope of one, investigated carefully the invention of a stranger to him, and gives a professional opinion thereon simply from the love of science and the public good. This invention opens a new theory of locomotion, which, if practical, cannot fail to come into use in many places. That it is practical can scarcely be doubted. It needs no argument to prove that a car will run down hill by its own gravity, if the hill is steep enough; nor will it need much argument to convince the educated mechanic that the elevator which is here used cannot fail to work. The principle involved is simply that of the Bramah (hydrostatic) press, adapted to elevating instead of compressing, and using air instead of water. This substitution of air for water, while it does not affect the power, is material for our use, because water has no elasticity and its action is slow, while the use of compressed air, on account of its great elasticity, would insure instantaneous action. That this elevator will work is not a matter of conjecture, for the principles governing it are well established in science. Being assured, therefore, that the motive power is reliable, we turn to its cost.

COST OF MOTIVE POWER.

The difference to be overcome on half mile sections of a road is ten and one-half feet of elevation. It is probable that the amount of elevation may be reduced below this point hereafter, but with this amount we are assured it will work.

The question which presents itself is, Can a given weight be hoisted ten and a half feet with greater ease and less expense than it can be hauled two thousand six hundred and forty feet? Manifestly, yes, for many reasons. To haul the weight, the motor must move with it, and its weight must be added to that of the body to be hauled, while for hoisting you can employ stationary power. Again, for hoisting, stationary intermittent power can be used, while for moving bodies we have already shown it cannot; the latent power, which is confined in one bulk and used occasionally for an effort in one case, is in the other divided amongst a hundred consumers, who exhaust it constantly. If it were necessary to exert the greatest possible economy in working this road, the air might be compressed by tidal wheels, or even by windmills, which power would cost nothing after the first cost of construction; but such rigid economy is not necessary, and as steam power is more reliable, and as one boiler and engine works the entire road, it would be better to use it. It is plain that the cost of operating this road will be a fractional part of the cost of any other plan.

THE ROUTE AND STRUCTURE.

When the best method of locomotion shall be fairly tried and approved by New York, many routes and roads will be required to supply the public need as well for cross-town as for lateral travel, but for immediate relief a central route is demanded connecting Harlem with the City Hall. With this view the following line is proposed, starting at City Hall Park and thence up Chatham street, Bowery and Third auenue, to Harlem bridge. Two tracks running north and two south, could be supported on a framework of iron columns consisting of three rows, one row on each sidewalk, and the third running down the centre of the street, all braced strongly together by girders across the street, and laterally to each other, the columns standing in line about thirty feet apart. The structure braced in this way, may be made exceedingly light and ornamental, because the weight to be sustained is but little; there is no jar, resistance, or wear, and the friction is hardly appreciable. It is doubtful if the noise made by a car passing could be heard in the street below. Should this plan be adopted the two inner tracks could have their stations one mile apart, for through travel, and the two outer ones every half mile apart for way travel, arranged alternately, thus giving a station every quarter mile. Or if it was decided at first to have but two tracks, the line of columns in the centre of the street could be dispensed with, and at each station two elevators could be used instead of one for each track, making a junction with the main track by switches which would operate alternately, and thus allow cars to be run every minute on one track, and still allow time for passengers to get in and out at the stations. Lamp-posts, telegraph-poles, and awning-posts could all be taken away from the streets, leaving only the uniform and graceful columns of the road which could be used as substitutes for all these purposes. The stations at the elevators, can be reached by tasteful spiral iron stairways leading up twelve and one-half feet, located at the street corners, or the second story of buildings can be used instead and a platform built out from the building to the track. There is another method of conveying a car from the foot of one inclined section to the summit of the next (other than by elevating it), and that is to build the track in successive long declines and short steep ascents, the car running down the decline by its gravity, and being dragged up the ascent by a short cable, to and over the head of the next decline, the distance of ascent to be as short as the elevation to be overcome will admit of. This arrangement is looked upon by the inventor as so greatly inferior to his method of elevating the car, for all purposes which now present themselves, that he only refers to it here, that hereafter he may claim, if desired, this arrangement of alternate declines and ascents.

AIR ENGINES AGAIN.

Now, although we have maintained that compressed air cannot be used as the sole power for running an engine on each car continuously, still, to use an air engine on each car, in connection with our system of inclines and elevators, would be far superior to all car-starting apparatus or lever movements of any kind, simply because the work for it to do is occasional, not constant. By a combination of this kind the grades of the inclines could be reduced materially, which would decrease the cost of construction, and increase, if desired, the length of the sections, thereby reducing the number of elevators. A few strokes of the air engine at starting, and an occasional stroke thereafter, would serve to keep up high speed on an incline with a grade much reduced below our table. It will be seen that it is the combination with the inclined plane which would give the detached air engine value as a motor. The engineer will concede this proposition,—as it is allowed :* "That the cost of draught on a railroad is nearly as the power employed, so that it will cost nearly twice as much to carry a load on a railroad with an ascending grade of twenty-five feet to the mile, as to carry it on a level route."

WOULD THE ROAD PAY?

In 1867 the number of passengers carried by the Third avenue road was 20,000,000, and by all the street roads about 102,000,000. For 1870, it is estimated that 150,000,000 will require transportation, and for 1880, over 250,000,000. Supposing this road for the first year carried only 20,000,000 passengers at six cents, it would on this business alone pay its expenses and divide seven or eight per cent. quarterly on its stock or its cost of construction. There can be no doubt but that it would pay.

IN THE COUNTRY.

It is not alone to elevated railroads in cities that this plan of locomotion is adapted. It can be used almost anywhere for travel where the distances between stations are short or

* See article in *American Artisan* of May 27, 1868, entitled "The Effects of Grades on Railway Expenses."

stoppages frequent, and where it is more desirable to run single cars at short intervals rather than heavy trains at long ones. For this purpose the cost of building a road would be small compared with its cost for city use, as the land could be bought or the right of way secured, and a great part of the elevation above the street thus dispensed with. This road is especially adapted to places where the land lies level, but even in places where considerable irregularity of surface exists it can be used to advantage, and the inventor believes that the easiest way to overcome an intervening hill, if it cannot be cut through or avoided, is to elevate the car above its crest, rather than drag it up a steep ascent. This assertion is a bold one, but for the present is so modified as to apply only to the locomotion of cars singly.

FOR BRIDGES.

No system of travel across long bridges connecting populous places could possibly be devised which would offer the advantages of this plan. The cost would be nominal, and the speed obtained would be such that a few cars would furnish means for large transportation. The tracks could be raised and supported at such a distance above the main floor of the bridge that they would in nowise interfere with its other travel. Horse cars on the bridge could be dispensed with, and the bridge would furnish to passengers all the comforts of a ferry, insuring swifter transportation and not subject them to the delays which ferries are liable to. A tidal wheel would compress all the air required to work the elevators, so that even the use of a steam engine could be dispensed with. The fare could be placed at one cent and the road would still pay handsomely.

CONCLUSION.

The subject of communication between place and place is an all-important one. The net work of railroads which have been established all over the United States within the last twenty years, proves that capital well understands their value.

On this subject there is no thought of economy, and it is probable that during the next decade the number of miles of road now laid will be more than doubled. The want of communication in New York city greatly retards its progression. Vast numbers of business men have been forced into Long Island and New Jersey who would otherwise have been residents of upper New York or Westchester county. Reliable and cheap means of going up town would undoubtedly soon people the whole island and double in value the land in the lower part of Westchester county. Is it too much for the inventor to say that he believes his plan of relief the best yet presented, and therefore asks for his improvement careful consideration, while he invites the most thorough criticism.

Respectfully,

ROBERT A. CHESEBROUGH,

132 *Maiden Lane, New York.*

NEW YORK, *December*, 1868.

www.ingramcontent.com/pod-product-compliance
Lightning Source LLC
LaVergne TN
LVHW011147110826
845150LV00008B/2551

9781418192457